P9-DET-591

CLASSIFYING ANIMALS

Why Am I a Bird?

Greg Pyers

Raintree
Chicago, Illinois

a division of Reed Elsevier Inc.
Chicago, Illinois

Customer Service 888-363-4266
Visit our website at www.raintreelibrary.com

For information, address the publisher:
Raintree, 100 N. LaSalle, Suite 1200, Chicago, IL 60602

Typeset in 21/30 pt Goudy Sans Book
Printed and bound in China by South China Printing Company Ltd

10 09 08 07 06
10 9 8 7 6 5 4 3 2 1

Library of Congress Cataloging-in-Publication Data
Pyers, Greg.
Why am I a bird? / Greg Pyers.
p. cm. -- (Classifying animals)
ISBN 1-4109-2014-3 (library binding-hardcover) --
ISBN 1-4109-2021-6 (pbk.)
1. Birds--Juvenile literature. I. Title.
QL676.2.P94 2006
598--dc22

2005012220

Acknowledgments
The author and publishers are grateful to the following for permission to reproduce copyright material: Alamy/Jan Baks: p. **17**; Heather Angel/Natural Visions: pp. **12**, **18**; APL/Minden Pictures: p. **10**, /Corbis/© Roger Tidman: p. **6**; © Jack Binch: p. **9**; Bradleyireland.com: p. **7**; Mike Lane/WWI/Still Pictures: p. **14**; © Arthur Morris/Vireo: p. **23**; Photolibrary.com/OSF: pp. **13**, **15**, /AnimalsAnimals: pp. **21**, **25–7**, /Peter Arnold: pp. **22, 24**; © TomVezo.com: pp. **8**, **19–20**. All other images PhotoDisc.

Cover photograph of a herring gull reproduced with permission of Photolibrary.com/AnimalsAnimals.

Every effort has been made to contact copyright holders of any material reproduced in this book. Any omissions will be rectified in subsequent printings if notice is given to the publisher.

The paper used to print this book comes from sustainable resources.

Contents

Words that are printed in bold, **like this**, are explained in the glossary on page 31.

All Kinds of Animals

There are millions of different kinds of animals. There are big animals, small animals, animals with feathers, and animals with scales (plates that cover the skin). There are animals that have sharp teeth, animals that have flat teeth, and animals that have no teeth at all.

But have you noticed that, despite all these differences, some animals are still rather similar to one another?

Snow geese are flying animals.

Sorting

Books are sorted on library shelves so that we can find the right one when we need it. Animals that are similar to one another can also be sorted into groups. Sorting animals into different groups can help us learn about them. This sorting is called **classification**.

This chart shows one way that we can sort animals into groups. Vertebrates are animals with backbones. Invertebrates are animals without backbones. Birds are vertebrates.

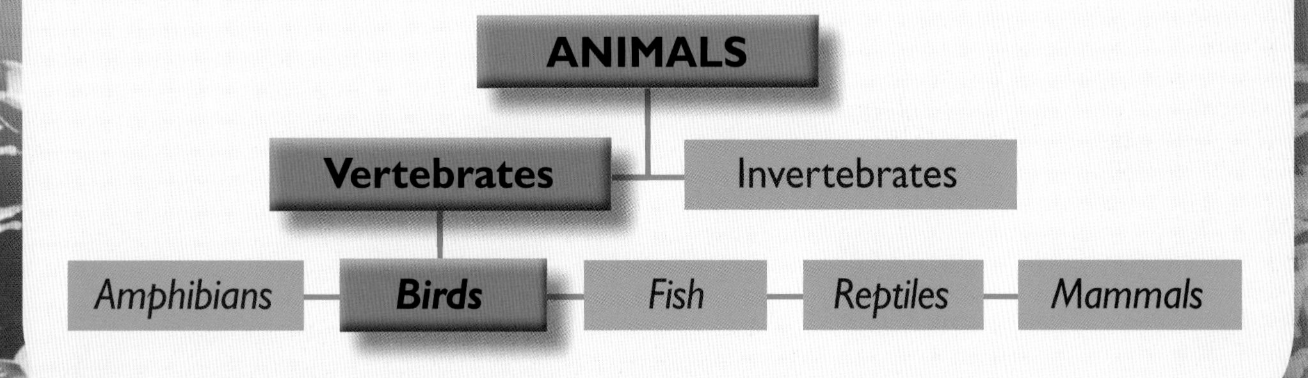

A Gull Is a Bird

Birds are one group of animals. Ostriches, sparrows, and parrots are birds. But why? What makes a bird a bird? In this book, we will look closely at one bird, the herring gull, to find out.

As you read through this book, you will see a ✔ next to important information that tells you what makes a bird a bird.

FAST FACT

There are about 9,200 different **species**, or kinds, of birds.

A herring gull has a white body, gray and black wings, a white tail, and pink webbed feet.

Gulls

There are many kinds of gulls. Gulls are noisy seabirds with **webbed feet** and strong **bills**. They live in areas near the sea all over the world.

Herring gulls

Herring gulls are found in many seaside towns from North America to Europe. They are medium-sized gulls, measuring about 24 inches (60 centimeters) from the tips of their bills to the ends of their tails. Herring gulls' calls can usually be heard throughout the day along the coast. To many people, these calls are a reminder of vacations at the beach.

Herring gulls gather together in large groups called flocks.

A Gull's Body

A herring gull has a solidly built body. A solid body helps this bird cope with the strong winds and wild weather of its **habitat** near the coast.

Feathers

Like all birds, a herring gull has feathers. The feathers on its head and body are short and soft. They grow thickly. The feathers on its wings are long and stiff. These are used for flying.

FAST FACT

Flightless birds, such as the emu, have more feathers than birds that fly. An emu's feathers are unusual. They have two main shafts, or stems, instead of one.

A herring gull has different types of feathers on different parts of its body.

Wings and legs

A herring gull has large wings. On the ground, the gull usually folds them neatly against its body. It has long, pink legs and **webbed feet**, like a duck's feet. Webbed feet help the gull to paddle when it lands on the sea to rest or feed. Sometimes a herring gull may lose a leg when a fish bites from below. Perhaps you have seen a one-legged gull.

A herring gull's webbed feet work like flippers under the water.

Inside a Gull

Inside a herring gull's body is a skeleton. The skeleton is made of many bones joined together. A layer of muscles covers the skeleton. Covering the muscles is the herring gull's skin.

Backbone

Running along a herring gull's back is a backbone. All birds have a skeleton and a backbone, which is made up of many small bones joined together. The backbone is very important because the herring gull's leg bones, wing bones, **skull**, and ribs are attached to it.

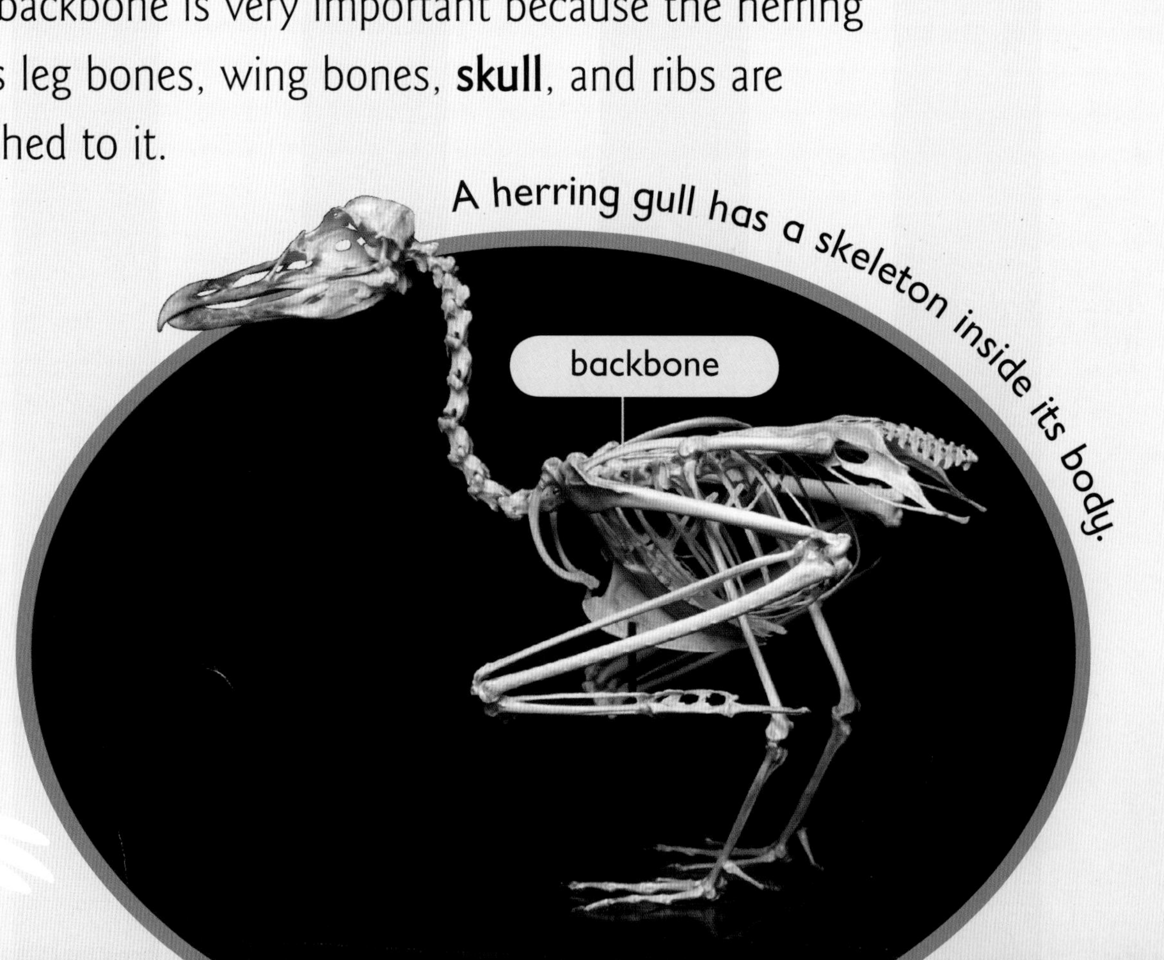

A herring gull has a skeleton inside its body.

Organs

There are **organs** inside a herring gull. These include a heart, a liver, a stomach, and **lungs**. The organs have important jobs to do.

FAST FACT

All birds have a heart with four separate sections called chambers.

Breathing

All birds have lungs and breathe air. A herring gull's lungs take in **oxygen** from the air. When a herring gull breathes through its nostrils, air moves into its lungs. From there, oxygen passes into the blood.

These are some of the organs inside a herring gull.

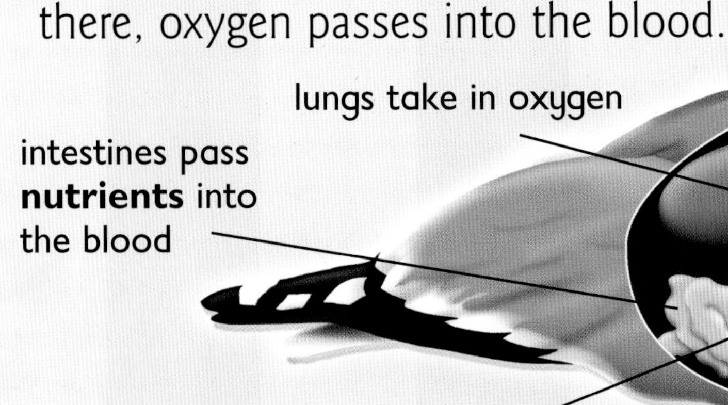

A Warm Body

A herring gull has a warm body, no matter what the air **temperature** is. A herring gull needs a warm body so that it can be active. All birds always have warm bodies, so they are often called warm-blooded animals.

Keeping warm

A herring gull's feathers keep it warm. Feathers trap warm air close to the herring gull's skin. The feathers on a gull's body grow very close together. This means they are able to trap the gull's body heat very well.

Feathers grow thickly over a herring gull's body.

Preening

Have you noticed how neat birds keep their feathers? A herring gull may spend an hour or more each day combing and straightening its feathers with its beak. This is called **preening**. Birds preen because body feathers trap heat best when they are kept in place. Feathers used for flying also work best when they are neatly in place.

FAST FACT

Gulls smear oil over their feathers. The oil keeps the feathers **waterproof**. It comes from a **gland** just above the bird's tail.

A herring gull also cleans its feathers while preening them.

Flying

Herring gulls are expert flyers. A herring gull's wings are long and narrow. This is an excellent shape for gliding on the wind. Herring gulls use their tails to help them change direction and to slow down when landing. When a herring gull is flying, its body makes a pointed shape in the air. This helps it to move through the air easily.

A herring gull's wingspan may be 38 inches (96 centimeters) from tip to tip.

A body for flying

To fly, a herring gull must be light enough for its wings to lift it off the ground. Herring gulls' bones have air spaces inside them. This makes them much lighter than the solid bones of mammals (another group of animals, which includes humans). Herring gulls have no teeth. Teeth are heavy. Instead, a herring gull has a **bill**, or beak. A bill is light but strong. ✔ All birds have beaks and no teeth. A fully grown herring gull weighs about 3 pounds (1.4 kilograms).

FAST FACT

Flightless birds, such as cassowaries and rheas, also have bones with air spaces in them. This means that long ago, these birds must have been able to fly.

bill

A herring gull's red-spotted bill is lightweight. This helps the herring gull to fly.

Food

Herring gulls eat a wide range of food. They have very good eyesight, which they use to search for food. They fly along beaches looking for fish and other animals washed ashore. Herring gulls often steal eggs from the nests of other seabirds. Their **prey** includes the chicks of other seabirds. Herring gulls also fly inland to feed on worms in plowed fields.

Herring gulls often visit garbage dumps to feed on food scraps.

Eating

Like all birds, a herring gull cannot chew its food because it has no teeth. Instead, it swallows its food whole. The food moves down the gull's throat and into its gizzard. The gizzard is an **organ** in the herring gull's chest. It grinds the food into small pieces. A herring gull swallows small pieces of gravel, which then sit in its gizzard. These help the gizzard to do its job.

FAST FACT

Raptors are birds with hooked beaks. Eagles, owls, buzzards, and hawks are raptors. These birds use their beaks to tear their food into smaller pieces for swallowing.

A herring gull will often swallow an egg whole.

Nesting

In spring, herring gulls come together in large numbers. Males and females form pairs. They call to each other, make stretching movements, and arch their necks in a kind of dance. This is called **courtship**. Courtship helps the birds in each pair to recognize each other. Many other bird **species** also make courtship displays.

Herring gulls form pairs before nesting.

Building a nest

Each pair of herring gulls now builds a nest. A herring gull's nest is made from a range of materials. Sticks, grass, weeds, moss, and even plastic bits of garbage may be used. Many herring gulls build their nests on cliffs. Others nest on flat ground. Herring gulls also build their nests in seaside towns. They may use window ledges or rooftops.

FAST FACT

Many birds, such as kookaburras, parrots, and toucans, nest in hollow branches or hollow tree trunks. Some birds, such as swallows, build their nests out of mud. Other birds, such as emperor penguins, do not build nests at all.

The male and female herring gulls share the jobs of building and looking after the nest.

Eggs

Like all bird **species**, herring gulls lay eggs. After each pair **mates**, the female herring gull lays two, three, or four eggs in the nest. The eggs have hard shells, just as all bird eggs do. Herring gull eggshells have a speckled pattern. This helps to hide the eggs from **predators**.

The color and pattern of herring gull eggs help to camouflage, or hide them.

Incubating

The **adult** herring gulls take turns sitting on the eggs. They do this to keep the eggs warm. This is called **incubating** them. Inside each egg, an **embryo** is growing. The embryos will become chicks—as long as the eggs stay warm.

Protecting eggs

Herring gulls protect their eggs against predators. Sometimes eggs are stolen and eaten by other birds, including other herring gulls.

FAST FACT

The mallee fowl is a large bird. The male builds a mound of leaves and soil, and then the female lays eggs inside it. As the leaves rot, they give off heat. This warms the mound and incubates the eggs.

A herring gull squawks loudly to scare predators away from its nest.

Chicks

The herring gull chicks hatch from their eggs after about 30 days. ✔ All birds hatch from eggs. The chicks are covered in **down** feathers that are brown and white. These colors are good camouflage. This means it is difficult for **predators** to see them. Even so, the chicks' parents must protect the chicks from other herring gulls that may snatch and eat them.

A herring gull chick looks different from its parents.

Feeding

The chicks cannot find their own food, so the parents bring food to them. They carry the food in a special pouch in their throats. This pouch is called a crop. When a chick wants to be fed, it pecks at the red spot on its parent's **bill**. The parent then opens its bill and brings up the food for the chick.

A herring gull must feed its chicks to help them grow and stay healthy.

FAST FACT

Cuckoos are birds that lay their eggs in another bird's nest. The other bird may be a robin. The robin **incubates** the cuckoo's egg. When the cuckoo chick hatches, the robin feeds it.

Growing Up

The herring gull chicks grow very quickly. A few days after hatching, they can walk. Their brown and white **down** feathers soon begin to fall out and **adult** feathers grow. When the chicks are about 36 days old, they have all their adult feathers. They are then ready to fly.

FAST FACT

Male and female herring gulls are the same color. In many bird **species**, males and females may be very different colors. For example, the male eclectus parrot is green with an orange beak. The female eclectus parrot is red and blue with a black beak.

A young herring gull often has some down feathers and some adult feathers.

Leaving home

The young herring gulls leave the nest as soon as they can fly. They will have to feed themselves from then on. They learn where to find food by following other herring gulls when they go out looking for food.

Herring gulls become adults when they are about three years old. They are then old enough to raise young of their own. A herring gull may live for 30 years.

Herring gulls may fly many miles in search of food.

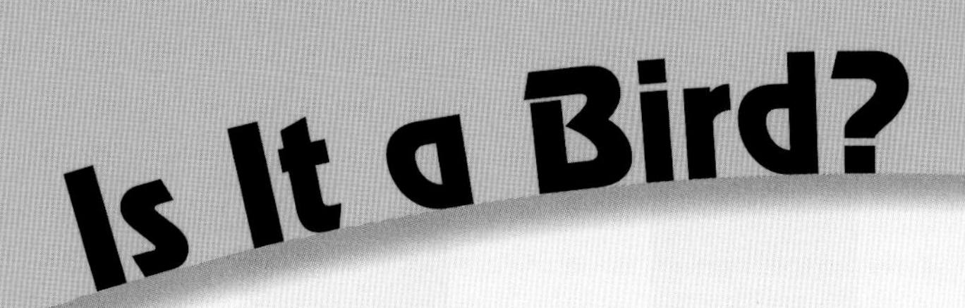

Is It a Bird?

A herring gull is a bird because:

- ✔ It has a backbone
- ✔ It has **lungs** and breathes air
- ✔ It hatches from an egg that has a hard shell
- ✔ It has a warm body
- ✔ It has feathers
- ✔ It has a beak (**bill**) and no teeth.

A herring gull is a bird.

Test yourself: little penguin

The little penguin lives in waters near the coasts of Australia and New Zealand. It feeds on small fish that it catches with its bill. It is a fast swimmer, using its flippers to push itself through the water. The little penguin has very short feathers, which keep it warm. It has a backbone and comes to the sea surface to breathe air into its lungs. Little penguins hatch from eggs laid by their mothers among rocks or in burrows in sand dunes.

Is the little penguin a bird? You decide.
(You will find the answer at the bottom of page 30.)

A little penguin's flippers and **webbed feet** help it to swim.

Animal Groups

This table shows the main features of the animals in each animal group.

Mammals	Birds	Reptiles
backbone	backbone	
skeleton inside body	skeleton inside body	skeleton inside body
most have four limbs	four limbs	most have four limbs
breathe air with **lungs**	breathe air with lungs	breathe air with lungs
most have hair or fur	all have feathers	all have scales
most born live; three **species** hatch from eggs; females' bodies make milk to feed young	all hatch from eggs with hard shells	many hatch from eggs with leathery shells; many born live
steady, warm body **temperature**	steady, warm body temperature	changing body temperature

Fish	Amphibians	Insects
backbone	backbone	no backbone
skeleton inside body	skeleton inside body	exoskeleton outside body
most have fins	most have four limbs	six legs
all have gills	gills during first stage; **adults** breathe air with lungs	breathe air but have no lungs
most have scales	no feathers, scales, or hair	many have some hair
most hatch from eggs; some born live	all hatch from eggs without shells	many hatch from eggs; many born live
changing body temperature	changing body temperature	changing body temperature

Find Out for Yourself

People who live near the coast in North America or Europe can see herring gulls all year round. Other parts of the world have different **species** of gulls. You can learn a lot about gulls, and other birds, by watching them. You can find books, called field guides, that will help you name the species of birds you see and hear in your local area.

For more information about herring gulls and other birds, you can read more books and look on the Internet.

More books to read

Dubois, Philippe J., and Valérie Guidoux. *Birds*. New York: Harry N. Abrams, 2005.

Richardson, Adele D. *Birds*. Mankato, Minn.: Capstone, 2004.

Savage, Stephen. *Birds: What's the Difference?* Chicago: Raintree, 2000.

Using the Internet

You can explore the Internet to find out more about birds. An adult can help you use a search engine. Type in a keyword such as *birds* or the name of a particular bird species.

Answer to "Test yourself" question:
A little penguin is a bird.

Glossary

adult grown-up

bill hard covering on a bird's mouth; a beak

classification sorting things into groups

courtship display that birds make when they are forming pairs

down soft, fluffy kind of feather

embryo very early stage in the growth of a chick inside its egg

gland part of the body that makes a liquid, such as sweat or milk

habitat place where an animal lives

incubate keep an animal warm

lungs organs that take in air

mate come together to make new animals

nutrient part of food that an animal needs to survive

organ part of an animal's body that has a certain task or tasks

oxygen gas that living things need to survive

predator animal that kills and eats other animals

preen comb and straighten feathers

prey animals that are eaten by other animals

skull all the bones of an animal's head

species kind of animal

temperature how warm or cold something is

waterproof does not let water get in

webbed feet feet that have skin between the toes

Index